RESCUED KITTIES

A Collection of Heart-Warming Cat Stories

L. G. Taylor & G.F. Klassen

Taylor & Klassen

Dedication

This book is dedicated to all the precious cats we have rescued over the years:

- Duran AND Duran (obviously two kitties of the 80's!)
- Cassandra
- Mickey
- Boris
- Natasha
- Shadow
- Nekko-Grace
- Brinkley

Taylor & Klassen

Table of Contents

Taylor & Klassen

Foreword

It gives us great pleasure to bring you this collection of true heart-warming stories of rescued kitties. When we put out the call for personal stories, we had no idea what would happen. What DID happen was the arrival of one heartfelt story after another --- and we knew we had something special to share.

This collection is a delightful representation of various cultures throughout the United States and Canada. In order to keep the "flavor" of each story, there has been minimal editing. These are true stories – written by the cat owners – with laughter, tears and love infused into each line.

We've so enjoyed reading these "slice of life" adventures of each battered, beautiful and much beloved rescued kitty. We trust you will too.

With gratitude,

L.G. Taylor and G.F. Klassen

Taylor & Klassen

Jack's Story

Wendy Wilwert
Platteville, WI

I wasn't looking for a new cat. Really, I wasn't. I had three already, and that was plenty, right? A single woman in my mid-thirties, I joked about being well on my way to becoming the proverbial crazy cat lady -- but it wasn't my intention to expand the collection any further, any time soon. I lived in a mobile home out in a somewhat rural area, where there were a lot of outdoor cats, ferals, and strays wandering about. My next-door neighbors kept a big dish of cat food on their porch, and, needless to say, it was a popular hangout for all the neighborhood felines. I enjoyed watching them romp around, and often would find one lounging on my porch or darting out from beneath it, but they all generally kept their distance from me, and would run off whenever I approached. I wasn't "their" human.

The winter of 2013-2014 was a rough one in southwest Wisconsin. It was bitterly cold, and I'll admit that I did worry about all those poor kitties out there. There wasn't much that I could do about it, though. There was a panel of the skirting on my house that was askew, and I left that as it was, allowing the neighborhood cats to at least crawl in beneath my house for some shelter, if they needed it. I felt better whenever I saw little paw tracks leading in and out through the snow, knowing that at least they had someplace to go that was out of the wind and the elements.

Spring came slowly and reluctantly, warming up a bit for a day or two at a time before reverting to cold once more. It was sometime in April or May when I noticed a new cat hanging around, a striped gray tabby guy that I didn't recognize. At first, I thought nothing of it. There were a lot of cats around. He was cute, of course – but aren't they all?

For a week or two I noticed him often on my porch, peeking in the windows at my other cats, gazing forlornly at me through the storm door. I'd laugh and tell him to go on home, he didn't live here, and we had quite enough furballs in the house for the moment, thank you. Being a cat, naturally, he paid me no mind… just gazed up at me, and sneezed. He had a pretty nasty cold, and while I felt awful for him, I didn't need any of my furkids getting sick!

As the weather warmed up enough to hang laundry outside to dry, he became my shadow whenever I went outside, following me to and fro, rubbing up against my ankles, flopping down in the grass, showing me his belly, mewing and sneezing in the most heart-meltingly adorable way. He'd even nonchalantly try to follow me right on into the house! Obviously, this was a domesticated cat. He'd been around people before, yet he didn't seem to have a home to go to – otherwise, why would he spend so much time around me?

I talked with the neighbors about him one day, and they said that they suspected that he had been dumped off at the side of the road nearby, and that it happened often near the end of the school year at the local university. Students were moving out and couldn't take the cat with them, so they'd leave it in the wild to fend for itself. My heart melted a little more. He was SUCH a sweet little guy! I just couldn't imagine anyone giving him up or not making sure he was going to a proper home!

He continued to be my little laundry helper, and would come running to greet me every afternoon when I came home from work. I was still quite convinced that three cats were plenty...but deep down, my resistance was weakening. The last straw came when the weather once again turned cold and wet, and I found him huddled under a table on my porch, wet and shivering. I just couldn't take it anymore. I scooped him up, put him in a carrier, and took him to a local pet hospital, where I asked them to check to see if he, by any chance, might be micro chipped. He wasn't.

Right away, I made an appointment for the following morning to have him checked over thoroughly. Then I took him home and put him in a spare room -- the one room where my other cats weren't allowed. I went out and picked up a new litterbox, food dishes, toys, and a little fleece blanket to snuggle up in. I took a soft piece of foam and wrapped it in some soft fabric and made him a little bed, then sat with him for a while, as he explored his new surroundings and got settled in. I don't think his little rumble-motor stopped running the entire time! The poor little guy was so clearly starved for affection and love. I knew, right then, that despite my best intentions... I had just adopted a new cat. Or perhaps... he had adopted me. I still haven't worked that out.

The next day, we went back to the pet hospital to do some tests, get some immunizations, and start him on some antibiotics for his cold, and cream for ear mites. The vet and vet techs all agreed -- he was the sweetest, most cooperative cat they had ever seen. The vet had to laugh when she went to listen to his heart and lungs with a stethoscope, and had to try to tune out his loud purring. He didn't even flinch when they drew blood or gave him shots, didn't fight over going into the carrier, and didn't resist taking the medications. I think it's the first time I didn't leave the vet with a few new scratches as the result of one of my cats expressing his or her displeasure with me.

No, this cat just loves and wants to be friends with everything and everyone. It was that facet of his personality that helped me choose his name. All of my pets have names that are related to science fiction shows. There's Tribble Tiberius and Kira Nerys (Rysie), with Star Trek names; and then there's Chloe Vera -- that one's a little more obscure. I took her in from a friend, so I didn't choose her first name, but her middle name is also the name of Jayne's very favorite gun, on Firefly. Looking at this sweet, purring little boy in my arms, so trusting and loving and desperate for affection from anyone and everyone, it didn't take more than a moment's thought to settle on Captain Jack Harkness, of Doctor Who and Torchwood fame. The name fit him to a T. The others put up a bit of a fuss at first, determined not to like the new invader in their territory, but I introduced them gradually, only letting them all be together when I was home to supervise. It took a remarkably short amount of time before I found Jack, Tribble, and Chloe playing and chasing one another around the house. Rysie is still determined to be stubborn and refuses to like him -- I think she's still mad at me for taking in Chloe, and she's been with us for three or four years, now! But deep down, I think even she is starting to soften toward him. The twinkle in his eye and the love in his heart is impossible to resist.

Jack

Jayke's Rescue

Vicky Mclaughlin
Squamish. B.C.

June 29th, 2013 I received a phone call from a friend of mine who rescues animals. I was asked if I could take in five kittens that were just a few days old. Their mother had been hit and killed by some kids on a quad. The following day my friend, D.R., knocked on my door with kitty formula and a kennel of five little kitties. Lilbit was the smallest one, no bigger than a little hamster.

I wasn't the only one who fell in love with these little ones. Jayke did too! Jayke is a golden retriever, German shepherd, Bernese mountain dog. He was just a little over a year old himself and had been around an older cat here and there, but never a group of kittens. The kitties were all from one litter, and the mom had been a Siamese cat. Blue was cream colored with blue eyes, Toothless was all black and reminded me of the dragon on "How to Train Your Dragon," so hence the name. She also had blue eyes. Bosco the grey striped had attitude, and Funnyface, the tortoiseshell kitty, just suited the name. All were a cute bundle of blue eyed fur babies.

Jayke took to the kitties right away and started mothering them, so to speak. I bottle fed them and he did everything else, from cleaning them to getting them to do their business. I was so amazed at how this was so natural to him. He knew what to do and did it. After each kitty was fed and cleaned up he would pick it up and put it in the basket where they slept. When the last one was fed and cleaned, he would put it in the basket and touch each one with his nose to count them and make sure they were all there. Lilbit was the runt of the litter and just so tiny. I knew in my heart that she would not live a long life. I think Jayke knew it as well, as he gave Lilbit more love and attention than the others. Mind you, he gave them all love and attention. When they were ready for soft food, Jayke would make sure that Lilbit ate her fair share and would nose her back to the dish when she was being bullied away by her siblings. I put puppy training pads down and they would do their business on it or close to it anyway. I purchased a kitty litter box and would put them in and watch them play in it at first. Then they would hop out and Jayke would get up and pick them up and put them back in. Within the day they knew what it was for. Jayke would pick them up and put them in the litterbox and make sure they did their business. At nap time and bedtime Jayke would pick them up and put them in their basket and touch each one with his nose and then they would all settle down and go to sleep. As they got bigger, my bed became the bed for all of us. Bosco, the grey striped one, had to be touching me when he slept. He would sleep against my back or by my leg. As long as part of him was touching me he was fine. The rest would sleep, cuddled up to Jayke. When the kitties were 8 weeks old, friends who had just lost their cat and were mourning over the loss, saw Blue. They fell in love with Blue right away. So Blue left our home and went to his new home and family. Jayke looked all over for 3 days and cried because he was missing a baby. I did not even stop to think at the time that this would happen. The other kitties cried for their sibling and would look all over. By day 4 it was back to normal and everyone was happy and playing together, sleeping and eating together. The kittens took a liking to Jayke's food, and Jayke would lay there until the kittens finished eating out of his bowl. Once they were done, Jayke would get up and go eat.

I had to go out of town for two days and D.R said she would look after the crew while I was gone. When I returned home, there was a message to call D.R. She answered the phone, and as soon as she heard my voice she started crying. Panic set in and I asked her what was wrong. She said Lilbit had not looked well and had not been eating or drinking. D.R. said she had held her to her chest all day giving her loves and trying to get her to drink, but Lilbit had passed away. I knew in my heart she would not survive very long, but we gave her lots of love and attention for the short little life that she had here. I told D.R that I didn't blame her and that it was okay and that I knew she would not have a long life due to the fact that she was just so tiny and did not grow very much at all. The next morning D.R brought Jayke and his kitties home and he cried and looked for his Lilbit. All I could do was hug him and cry with him. For days, then weeks, I enjoyed watching Jayke and his babies play and nap together. They always made me laugh. They still do. There was no way I could tear this family apart again. They loved Jayke and

Jayke loved them. So Toothless, Bosco and Funnyface were off to the vet to be fixed and have their shots. Jayke cried all day and was in a panic because he could not find any of his babies. Even going to play and on walks was a job to get him out because he needed to find his babies first. Today Jayke and his babies are happy, healthy, and loving our new condo up here is Squamish. The kitties are happy hanging out on the deck, as this is the first time they have been outdoors. They are strictly indoor cats and the deck is as far as they go. They all still sleep, eat, and play together. Toothless very seldom meows. She likes putting her ears back and growls and snarls at people and other animals that walk by. Even if company comes over she will growl until she gets to know you. I don't think she knows she is a cat.

Yes, they are all my kids, and we are a very happy family.

Jayke & his Kitties

Funnyface, Toothless, Jayke, & Bosco

Boots Easter Miracle

Linda Wallis
Wingate, NC

Once upon a time in a neighborhood filled with flower gardens, large oak trees, and all types of friendly critters, there lived a Bengal kitty named Boots, our neighborhood jester. With a walk and run that was different than any other cat we had ever seen, his legs looked like he's walking on sticks. Boots was our neighbor's family cat from across the street. He always seemed to be compelled to come over to our house. We had fellow cats that he would play and fight with all time.

Over time, after all the disagreements between Boots and Cricket, one of our family cats, he insisted on being included in our family. And so he was. After two years had passed by, he had settled in as our family pet. Time would escape while rocking on the front porch watching him because he had this explosive personality that was so entertaining

One winter morning Boots heard the children laughing and playing outside, and he decided to join in on the fun. Walking and running up and down the slopes of snow and ice, he played with the kids all day. As we were heading out to take care of our daily errands, we never thought for one second that would be our last day to see our playful Boots. The next morning we felt something was amiss, because our jester was nowhere to be seen. As the days went by, we feared the worst. Many thoughts crossed our minds as to what could have happened.

Now spring had sprung. It was a beautiful Easter Sunday and we were headed to our local hardware store to pick up a few more items for our newly installed fence. For some reason, we were all thinking about Boots that day, and wishing that we could just know what happened to our family pet. As we were passing a patch of woods we saw a cat lying curled up alongside of the woods close to the highway. Our thoughts were, could it be our Boots? But we didn't get our hopes up.

We turned the car around, all the while feeling nervous that this cat might be him. As we got closer we could see the marble markings and white chest. It was our Boots! We called out to him and he stood up and looked at us. He cried and took a few steps in our direction. We couldn't believe what we were seeing. He could barely stand or even meow, but he managed to walk over to us and collapse in front of us. "Our Boots". Not knowing if he would live or die, we rushed him to the car, praying he would make it. After months of searching for him, the agony of losing him would be too much. We rushed back home to nurse him back to health.

Our drive seemed like forever even though we were less than half a mile from home. We laid his tired and boney body on the carpeted floor, where he was greeted by the rest of the family. Everyone was so surprised and excited that he was still alive and safely back home. We vowed to never let him roam outside by himself again. We will never know his full adventure or the trials he went through, all of those long days by himself. He waited for us near the highway close to our house, hoping we would spot him. Three months have passed, and now he's in perfect health. Boots is happy and back to being our cheerful jester. We choose to believe that there was a reason he was found on Easter Day. But we will leave that up to you to decide.

Boots

Taylor & Klassen

Amelia, the Half-Tailed Wonder

Kayla Reeves
Parker, CO

I have always thought of myself as a cat person. Growing up, my mother and I had various cats, all of which were rescued in some form or another. It began with a brother and sister pair she adopted from a shelter when I was just a baby. As long as I can remember, we've always had cats. Our most recent family cat, Patches, finally passed away at the ripe old age of 16 from Diabetes complications. She had spent the last few months of her life living with my husband and me. Since I was just about to finish my degree in Veterinary Technology, it made sense for me to take her in.

Even though Patches mainly kept to herself, when she passed, it felt as though something was missing. Since we had been cat people (with the exception of my husband who HATES cats), I felt as though we should make a trip to the local human society, and adopt another cat; perhaps an adult or senior cat who would otherwise not get adopted. I was even open to a special needs cat due to the nature of my career. We searched and searched, but none of the cats available really caught our eye. After listening to my husband go on and on about how much he disliked cats, I jokingly made the statement, "If you can find a cat-sized dog,

I'll consider it". We left with Hamilton, an older Silky Terrier. So much for the cat.

Almost a year had passed. We had in the interim adopted another small dog in July, and our beloved rescue pit bull, Vayda, had passed away that November. We were down to 3 dogs, two guinea pigs, fish, and a cat. This particular cat, Sinsow, was an owner surrender of a client at my clinic who was unable to care for him any longer. Sinsow was a very sweet cat, but so dependent that he nearly tripped me down the stairs at 5 months pregnant. My husband had recently deployed, and I decided that Sinsow needed a friend, because I wasn't going to have "death by lonely cat" as my end.

Instead of driving to the human society and attempting to spend any real time searching for another cat with my then 3-year old daughter, I decided to look online. What a concept. I spent a few weeks looking at the different cats they had available, and one cat in particular kept coming back to mind. Her name was Umma (later to be changed to Amelia). She had been an owner surrender due to a move. Best part: no adoption fee. I thought to myself, "There's probably something wrong with her". They had only posted photos of her face, it was really hard to tell what she truly looked like. The next day, my daughter and I made a trip to the humane society.

At our humane society, they have a few rooms where they house cats. They have a front room that houses some cats, mainly special needs, small animals and reptiles.

Umma/Amelia was in this room. I noticed her in a bottom kennel. An older woman approached the kennel, and the cat hissed at her. I thought, "Now I know why she's free". My daughter spotted her, and immediately ran up to the kennel. Before I could pull her back and say not to approach her, my daughter already had her fingers in between the bars. As I winced waiting for an attack – nothing happened. I looked, and the cat was meowing and rubbing up against the bars. Most cats would act that way with the old woman and hiss at the child, but not this cat. As I approached, her meowing and wanting attention increased. I finally could get a full look at her: gray and white (like my first two cats), with a notch out of her left ear, and this weird, half tail with a crook in the top. My daughter looked and me and said, "Mom, I want this one". I asked if she wanted to look at any other cats, and there was a stomping of a foot and a resounding "NO". Okay. I guess we'll take this one out to meet.

We went through the usual process – find a kennel attendant, "We want this one", etc. When we met with Umma/Amelia in the meet-and-greet room, it was clear she had chosen us, however I don't think she understood what she was getting herself into. About a half hour later, and an update on her story (owner surrender, was adopted then returned a few hours later) we were the proud owners of yet another rescue animal. I swear I could run a zoo. We brought her home, not knowing what to expect. We followed all of the "introduction instructions" given to us by the humane society, and after a few days, she began to really come around. She didn't mind the dogs, and was a little wary

19

of our other cat, but seemed to be doing ok. The next few months passed, and everyone seemed like they were getting along for the most part – Amelia was not a fan of Sinsow's antics, but seemed to tolerate him ok.

We adopted Amelia in January. We purchased a home and moved in June. Since she didn't have a hard time adjusting at our other home, we figured we would be ok at the new one. Boy were we wrong.

It began with this awful horrible meow/yowl before we went to sleep. Almost like she didn't want to be downstairs alone with Sinsow. We would hear fighting in the middle of the night. I attributed the behavior from both cats to stress from the move, however as time went on, things got worse. I decided to put a bell on Sinsow so we could figure out who was causing the trouble, and so Amelia could hear him coming. All it did was add music to the already screaming matches going on at night. Sinsow increasingly became aggressive towards Amelia, and Amelia was becoming increasingly aggressive towards us. Never towards our then new baby or daughter, but to my husband and me. We had to make a decision. Which cat got to stay, and which one had to go. Even though Sinsow at the time was more affectionate, he began marking all over our new house. That was a death sentence by my husband. We found Sinsow a new home and hoped that the removal of him would change Amelia's behavior.

By this point, Amelia had earned herself a place on my husband's "black list". She had hissed, struck out at, etc.

towards him. If he had had his way, both cats would have been gone. I told him to give her a chance now that the other cat wasn't here. We'll see how she does. If she continues to be a devil cat, then she'll go too. Luckily for her, and for us, she did a complete 180. She began to be sweet with me and the dogs again right away. My husband on the other hand would have stand-offs with her. Nothing ever resulted in injury, but the two of them would stare at each other likes dogs over a bone. It was ridiculous, and in good cat fashion, very dramatic. Fast-forward a few weeks, and she began to rub on his leg, and jump into his lap. We had discussed finding her a new home before our next move (this time to Europe), since she hadn't coped well with moving the first time. Maybe a single woman, or someone who could make her the center of their world. It was around this time that she began to "love up" on my husband. Like she was trying to show us why she should stay. I then told him, "She already is the center of someone's world – our daughter's, and unless you want to explain why she doesn't get to keep her cat, but all the dogs get to stay, then be my guest". It was very shortly after that that we realized we couldn't part with her. Our once feral, bug-catching, fat house cat with the ugly tail and partial ear was here to stay. She has gone from being an animal we thought we couldn't deal with, to a completely different cat. She's loving, and patient, and is great with our infant son. She loves to be the center of attention – she's a lap cat, and loves to snuggle under the blankets. She follows us all over the house, and doesn't like to be alone. She loves us, and wants to be with us, and I wouldn't trade that for the world. Amelia has also opened my husband's eyes to what great a pet a cat can be. He still swears once she passes no more cats, however, I still catch him with her in his lap.

Amelia

Rosie's Persistent Human Rescue

Deb R. Brimer
Mesquite, TX

I'm not sure whether I rescued Rosie or Rosie rescued me.

When Rosie came into my life, I was a self-professed "dog person". Unlike some dog people, I didn't dislike cats. I had just never experienced that special spiritual connection with feline creatures – or "cat love" – until Rosie came along.

My only personal cat encounters occurred as a child growing up in a once rural area of Mesquite, Texas, which was a favorite regional dumping ground for unwanted cats. Though I played with the feral cats and kittens – and on one occasion cared for a litter after a pack of large dogs mauled its mother to death – I quickly learned about the transient nature of undomesticated animals. They often disappeared as quickly as they came.

The overall pet culture in the late 1950s and 1960s wasn't much better. Essentially people lived indoors and animals lived outdoors. Between scorching Texas summers, cold winters and lack of proper pet care as we know it today, the life span of domestic animals was relatively short. Every time we buried a family pet, my mother, a half-breed American Indian, instilled a warning: "If you cry when an

23

animal dies, something bad will happen to a person you love."

The pattern for pet mortality in my family – coupled with my mother's harsh words – impacted me dramatically. I eventually developed a severe phobia of even the smallest dogs, which was likely secondary to the fear of my mother's admonition. After all, at the rate our pets bit the dust, my tears could have easily wiped out my entire family!

But love has the power to eventually teach old dogs new tricks.

I put Mom's prophecy behind me when I discovered the spunky schnauzer breed. Over more than three decades, I shed rivers of tears every time one of my aging dogs went to the Rainbow Bridge. And amazingly, my entire family lived through them all.

In many ways, I think my last two schnauzers – Zak and Annie – prepared me for Rosie. As diabetics that required an enormous amount of one-on-one care over nine-years, I gained a much broader understanding of my responsibility to God's creation. I'm convinced that God put Rosie in my life so that I could give her a loving home.

When Rosie showed up on the doorstep of our small office building, which was next door to my old home place in Mesquite, she was only about a year old and had just been abandoned. The lady who had bought the house after my Mom's death became a victim of the foreclosure crisis in 2006. When she vacated the home, she left Rosie behind, although she did leave a couple of windows open for Rosie to have shelter – at least for a while.

As I recount those days now, I get a much greater sense about how frightened and confused Rosie must have been. Yet in the midst of her insecurity, she consistently exercised animal wisdom and persistence at every turn.

Initially we cared for Rosie's basic needs by making sure she had plenty of food and water. At the end of the workday, she reciprocated by following us home, which was just around the corner. When we opened the front door each morning, Rosie was sitting on the porch waiting for her breakfast. Despite her young age, she quickly grasped our daily routine. By the time we got to the office, she was always there – waiting on us.

I'll never forget the first day Rosie walked inside the office. She marched passed me and disappeared down the hall like she knew precisely where she was going. As I watched that little ball of white and black fur take command of our office, she reminded me of a feline version of my mother whose name was Rose. So Rosie instantly became Mom's namesake, which seemed fitting since they shared a prissy, petite demeanor and had both lived in the same house.

For six months, Rosie was as faithful as any puppy dog I had known as she followed us back and forth to work each day. Clearly she had adopted us while all we had done was buy a few bags of cat food. But we had a laundry list of reservations about adopting Rosie. Aside from knowing nothing about cats, we were concerned about how well

Rosie, Zak and Annie would coexist – especially since Zak was blind from end-stage diabetes and neither had ever been around cats.

Old Man Winter was the deciding factor. In order to protect Rosie from the chilling temperatures lurking around the corner, we moved her into the office where she lived for five years. As animal lovers, we had the best of both worlds – loving pets at home and a loving pet at work.

I've heard that "you don't know a person until you live with them." The same can be said for cats.

Horror stories we had heard about cats likely contributed to our hesitance at making the adoption commitment. While Rosie seemed extremely sweet natured outdoors, what if she became a cat from hell indoors? I'm not sure if the office solution was a trial or a stair-step process. Nevertheless it paved the way for one of the most beautiful relationships we've ever known with one of God's creations.

From the moment Rosie moved in, she became *my* cat. Though she eventually perched herself on almost everything in the office – from windowsills and desks to every chair throughout the small building – her favorite spot was my lap. There I learned about that kneading thing that cats do with their claws. But the red marks on my legs were small things in comparison to that precious little face that looked up at me with such enduring love.

Since I was the sole creative department for our magazine, I normally spent countless night and weekend hours alone when the publication was in-production. For me, Rosie's companionship during those long, grueling hours provided the company of another living breathing being, which was comforting. For Rosie, my presence minimized the time she spent alone, as well as the mornings she felt it necessary to yell at me in cat talk when I arrived late to work.

During one marathon work stretch, I became extremely exhausted and decided to curl up on the wicker loveseat and take a short nap. When I awoke, Rosie was curled up on top of me – something I later learned was her modus operandi.

Our world changed in 2010. Between the financial devastation of The Great Recession and the industry demise of print media, I closed our company after 38 years in business and took Rosie home. Since Annie was still living, Rosie lived in a separate area of the house until Annie's death months later.

Suddenly Rosie became our "only child". While she didn't replace Annie, she did help ease the gut wrenching grief. Rosie settled into her new environment like she adapted to living at the office. She seemed grateful to have a home and be surrounded by love.

I continue to marvel at Rosie's low maintenance care, which simply consists of a clean litter box, fresh food and water, catnip and scratch toys, plenty of Temptations treats and a soft pillow to lay on.

I am still Rosie's pillow. The minute I lie down to rest for the night, Rosie gently takes her place on my chest where she places her left foot on my shoulder and gazes affectionately into my eyes as if she's reaching out to the depth of my soul. Then she rolls over on her left side, wraps her right leg around me and goes peacefully to sleep. For obvious reasons, I'm thankful that she's still a petite eight pounds. But I'm equally thankful that God blessed us with such a sweet gift.

I still don't know much about cats, which is perfectly fine because Rosie doesn't appear to fit the profile of most cats. Since I was "cat challenged" from day one, I trained Rosie in the same manner that I trained my dogs. As a result, she greets me at the door when I get home; she frequently follows me around; she's always affectionate; and she comes running when I give her the "come" command. (Okay, the last one doesn't always work. But rattling the box of Temptations treats never fails).

Thanks to Rosie's persistent human rescue, she has her forever home and I have my sweet natured Pretty Kitty to love, as well as a deeper insight into the animal kingdom. If dogs are man's best friend, I'm certain that precious cats are woman's best friend.

Rosie

Taylor & Klassen

Cat Tales

Stacy Lininger
Seaside, CA

It was the Fourth of July, seven years ago, when I heard crying kitty sounds outside my door amidst the fireworks. I saw a little strawberry blond kitty quivering under the bushes, but it wouldn't come to me. Then I saw another exactly like it. After several minutes of coaxing, they finally decided they were more afraid of the fireworks than of me, so I was able to get them to come inside. Their tiny little ribs were sticking out and they were clearly emaciated. I had no cat food, but I had just gone grocery shopping so I fed them turkey sausage. One of them, (probably Pumpkin), ate so fast, he threw up. I let them out around midnight when the fireworks were over and then went to bed. The next morning I opened the back door and there they were with their sister, a grey tabby with strawberry blond markings. They were looking at me as though they had suitcases in their paws and were saying – "We chose you!"

I had no interest in three baby anythings, but I knew these three were mine. I had just broken up with my boyfriend in the bay area and wouldn't be traveling as much so, why not? I welcomed them into my home, fed them well, and watched them grow. I never had a litter before and it was quite an experience. They would cuddle together, bite each other's fleas and sometimes cuddle with me and even try to bite my fleas. I had an instant family drop from the sky.

They each had a unique personality which is the only way I could tell the two boys apart. Putty was the alpha, although Pumpkin resented that, and constantly challenged him. Sissy was the little sis who let them sit on her and eat her food and never meowed or complained. She did hide a lot and I had to put a bell on her. Putty liked to dress up and was on the cover of a magazine called "Petcentric". The featured story was about pets who liked dressing up. He was the only cat in the midst of dogs and loving it. He also won $100 in a photo contest dressed up as a princess. He was quite a character.

Putty

I awoke one morning and could not find Pumpkin anywhere. I went into a panic and finally found him in the laundry room lying behind the washer. He wouldn't come out so I got a broom to chase him out. I was so annoyed that he had frightened me by his absence. Obediently he hobbled out, screeching all the way. Now I was really in panic mode. It turned out that his leg was broken, and I think he had been hit by a car. I took him to the vet and $1500 later he was pretty much as good as new. He died a few months later from a stone in his bladder as we were on the way to the vet. I found out boy cats are prone to that and it's a quick death. I remember holding his lifeless little body in my arms and seeing the peaceful look on his face. After all of these years of worrying I was going to lose one of them, I finally did, and it wasn't so horrible. He taught me not to fear death with that look on his little face. I buried him in the backyard, lowering his stiff body by hand and it wasn't morbid at all. Putty was angry though and took it out on me for a while by throwing a floor lamp on me and biting at my scalp. I finally had a talk with him and he left me alone and picked on his sister instead. I had another talk with him and he started to play with his sister like he had with Pumpkin. She soon found her voice and began to quietly meow.

Putty was the hunter in the family and once stalked a gopher for three months until he finally got it and proudly brought it inside for me to see. It scared the heck out of me and I had to have a neighbor remove it. It was as big as he was. He also was our protector, and once when I left the keys in the front door after bringing in groceries, he stood on his hind legs and hit the keys loudly against the door so that I would know. Putty left us a year later, dying suddenly of shortness of breath. I tried to take him to the vet but he ran from me and I finally found him under the tire of my car with his tongue sticking out as though he had been poisoned. It was like he had to be with his brother.

Sissy watched me bury him in the backyard next to Pumpkin and didn't seem sad at all. She then begin meowing up a storm, became very possessive of me and turned into a huntress. She was the last cat standing and ecstatic about it. It was her time.

She is now all three cats rolled into one, and a wonderful spirit. She talks smack like Putty, hunts birds and mice, and looks out for me like you wouldn't believe. She is the only cat I ever had who kisses. I put my head down to her and she raises hers and kisses me. Sometimes she will come up to me for a kiss. She stays close to home, unlike the boys, and is always there when I need her. The boys died young, but it was almost like they just came along to stake out a home for Sissy since they knew they would be moving on to their next life. This Fourth of July I will be celebrating the anniversary of when these angels appeared on my doorstep. Never let angels pass you by.

Sissy

SOMETIMES

Veronica Whitmore
Vancouver, WA

More often than not, you go to the pet store, or to the pound, and you choose an animal to take home with you. You plan ahead, you save your money, and you prepare by purchasing pet food and supplies. Usually, you plan to get a pet. Usually, you get a pet on purpose.

But sometimes, a pet that you didn't even know you wanted just appears in front of you and chooses you to be its person. Sometimes, you are needed by a homeless or abandoned animal, and you find yourself with an animal that picked you. Sometimes, you get a pet by accident.

That is what happened to me; I got a kitten by accident.

In the fall of 2011, when the leaves were falling and the nights were getting cold, I got home from work to find a small black kitten sitting on my front porch. She appeared to be waiting for me, but she wasn't mine. She was at the front door, white paws on the threshold, black tail wagging left to right, like a dog waiting to come in from the yard. I didn't want a cat; I'm allergic to cats. I shooed her off the porch, and as she went traipsing across my yard with leaves crunching under her feet, I went inside and forgot about her.

The next morning, in a rush to get out the door on time for work, I almost stepped on the small black kitten sitting on my front porch. She was still waiting for me, even though she wasn't mine. She was, once again, at the front door, head tilted, tail wagging. I laughed, but I didn't feed or pet her. I didn't want a cat, and I know that stray cats stick around if you dote on them.

When I got home from work that evening, this stubborn kitten was still on my porch. She was waiting patiently, tail gently wagging left to right, whiskers twitching. It was cold. I knew she must be cold, and the nights were only getting colder. Rather than shoo her off into the leaves again, I scooped her up. Nuzzling into my chest, she began to purr, and before I was even able to put down my bags, this little black kitten had crossed her paws over her eyes and dozed off.

Sometimes, you get a pet by accident.

I needed to find her home. She was too clean and groomed to have been away long, and too small to have survived many cold nights on her own. Her people must be missing her. So off I went, sleeping kitten in my arms, knocking on doors up and down the block. Neighbors sympathetically shook their heads, not knowing where she came from. One neighbor said he'd been feeding her and had even put a bed out for her on his porch. "But she eats and runs," he said with a grin, "she hasn't slept here once."

When it started getting dark, I headed home, still holding a sleeping kitten who surely believed by now that she wasn't sleeping outside tonight. I begrudgingly knocked on one last door, hoping for a miracle; I didn't want a cat. "Oh, yes, I know where she belongs," my elderly neighbor told me, "that couple up the way, about 5 blocks that way, they got her for their son about 2 weeks back." She went on to explain that the parents had gotten their son a kitten, and then the kitten had gotten out fairly quickly. Instead of looking for her, they replaced her. "When this kitten came home, they turned her away," my neighbor told me, shaking her head. Poor baby; they'd just dumped her. Still, I didn't want a cat.

I felt better about leaving her outside, knowing that a neighbor was feeding her, but it was pretty chilly. I walked back to his house and set her in the bed he'd left out, hoping she'd realize her good fortune and make a home there with him and his family. She sat on the bed, tail wiggling left to right, eyes wide, as I headed towards my own home. But for the first time since I first saw her, I wasn't quite so certain about not wanting a cat.

Sometimes, you get a pet by accident.

I decided that if she was back on my porch the next morning, I'd let her inside and look for a home for her. Surely if I posted her photo online, I could find a friend who wanted her; she was adorable and tiny. Headed to bed that night, I hoped she'd stayed on the neighbor's porch, where she would be cared for, or at least given a meal every day and a fluffy bed on which to rest.

Not only was she there in the morning, tail wagging, paws on the threshold like my house was her house, but she was still there after work, as though she hadn't moved a muscle for ten hours. "Alright," I shrugged, "come on in." I opened the front door and in she pranced, like she'd lived there for years. She did a few laps of the living and dining rooms, sniffed around the kitchen floor, then sauntered to the wall cadet heater in the living room, stretched, yawned, and laid down. Within moments, she was asleep, warm air blowing at her backside. And there she slept. She was there when I drove frantically to the store for pet food and a bowl, nail clippers, and a litter box set up. She was there while I cooked and ate my dinner, and she was there when I headed to bed.

But when I woke up in the morning, she was curled up in a tight ball, sleeping soundly on the floor next to my bed. I had gotten a pet by accident. I'd never wanted a cat, but now I wanted this cat. There she was, asleep on the floor beneath my side of the bed, content and warm. She had picked me.

That morning, I didn't have to work. Despite my intention to post her picture online and find her a forever home through my social network, I instead found myself in the car, abandoned kitten in my lap, driving to the vet. I had her examined, groomed, and micro chipped, and – after a pregnancy scare during her exam – I scheduled to have her spayed a few days later.

I named her Juno, after Ellen Page's character in the movie, because she was young and adorable like the Juno in the movie, and also because the vet had mistakenly told me she was pregnant. The name made more sense initially, when I thought my new kitten was going to be a teen mother, but it stuck even after the pregnancy news turned out to be a false alarm.

This little black kitten, with her white paws and long whiskers, had picked me; I was her person and she was my pet, and it would seem I had no choice in the matter. I got a pet by accident, after I rescued the tiny black kitten that stood her ground on my front porch until I caved.What I have learned about rescuing an animal that is otherwise homeless or abandoned, is that animals provide unconditional love in any way they know how. Juno is now three years old; she is chubby and has asthma, and a bad hip that keeps her from jumping onto the kitchen counters. She loves to sit in front of the patio door in the sun, but she loves nothing more than to curl up behind my knees, under a blanket. I didn't set out to bring a cat home, but instead I accepted that this cat was just going to make my home her forever home. I may have never wanted a cat, but I certainly love my little Juno. She's the cat that I got by accident.

Juno

The Rescue of Cosho

Kathleen Martino
Rowlett, TX

Cosho was not your typical Burmese cat. He was left out in the elements to fend for himself, and this was definitely not his forte. He had long white hair with black tips on the ends and a black nose. His long hair was dirty and matted and dry-looking, but he had a quality about him. He had a look of innocence and hope in those beautiful bright golden eyes. He was not a wild cat. Quite the contrary. He was sweet, in spite of his situation. He was lost and confused, looking for someone to love and to love him.

Cosho was just a baby at the time we met. I am not sure what happened in his young life or what happened to his mother. He had all the right markings to be a show cat. One very unique thing about Cosho was that he thought he could talk to humans. Quite a talker he was. You would ask him what he thought of the president, or any question for that matter, and he would sit and stare at you and talk for about a minute straight and stop. Not quite a meow, but a yep yep yep sound moving his head back and forth, and he continued no matter what you asked him. He loved riding in the car and lying across my shoulder talking to me and kissing me as we drove down the street. When you called for him, he would come running like a dog. But like a cat, he would get close enough to jump in your arms, talking all the time he was running toward you as if he were telling you all about his adventures that day.

Cosho was very skinny at the time we met and very undernourished, but seemed to be a very happy natured, trusting and loving creature. His ribs, in spite of his long hair, were showing, and he was very small for his age. He was a little bit of nothing.

Cosho had a friend...my cat, Bianca. Now Bianca on the other hand, is a very spoiled white-as-snow long haired, green eyed, beautiful Persian. She strolls through the neighborhood like she owns it. She reminds you of a rich spoiled beauty like that of a runway model; a bit stuck up and she thinks she is the queen bee. Bianca's disposition, to say the least, is that of a tiger; very assured of herself. All the other cats in the neighborhood know her. Although she is a fighter, she has a sweet and lovable side to her.

Now when Cosho showed up in the neighborhood it was not at all the welcome I think he was expecting. He was welcomed by the neighborhood bully. His name was Buster, an extremely large male cat who thought the neighborhood was his and his alone to run, and he was not about to let another male into his territory. This is how Cosho came into my life and was rescued.

So as the story goes, Cosho met up with Buster on the sidewalk one fine hot Texas summer morning, and this was not a pretty sight. Cosho was such a naïve, sweet little thing, and he did not understand why this Buster character was hissing and snarling at him. He looked puzzled and had no idea that he had to defend himself, or for that matter knew how to defend himself. The fight was on, and poor little Cosho was so weak and small he was not winning this fight at all. As I went running out the front door, leaving it open to save him and to get Buster off of him, along came Ms. Queen Bianca to the rescue. She cleared the stairs in two jumps, twisted her body and turned the corner with the ease of an acrobat in flight, and passed me like I was standing still. All I could see was a flash of white fur running by me. In an instant she came to Cosho's rescue. With her head down, Bianca hit Buster with a fierce blow and had him measured precisely. She resembled a lioness running after her prey. Buster rolled across the sidewalk and off of Cosho like a pill bug tumbling several times down the sidewalk. With fierce determination in her eyes and stature, Bianca turned and looked at Cosho as if to say: "RUN little guy, Run"!! -similar to a mother protecting her own. Cosho had a stunned, frightened and confused look on his face, not understanding what had just happened to him. He took off running as fast as he could and the fight was over.

As I watched in amazement, Bianca flew with the grace of the wings of angels to the top of the fence right above Buster and Cosho. Bianca was looking down on Buster and snarling and hissing. Her ears were laid back and her eyes looked like small slits. Her tail was puffed so big and swaying like a limb in a fierce thunderstorm. She was looking and growling at Buster as if she was saying, "You need to go on your way big boy and leave my little friend alone!" After a time, Buster walked off slowly, looking back a few times, contemplating something. What it was, I could only surmise. Although it was very clear that he was not happy about being defeated.

Well I looked and walked the neighborhood for hours looking for Cosho. I could not find him. I looked and called "Kitty! Kitty!" off and on all day - worried about him. Around 9:00 pm that evening, I was sitting on my bed thinking about Cosho and wondering if he was safe. I kept thinking about Buster and hoping no other Busters got the best of him. As I was contemplating all of this, I heard a shuffling noise under my bed, and there was this little head peeking out from under the bed with the bed skirt on the top of his head. It was Cosho, looking up at me and talking to me, as if he were saying: "Is it safe to come out? I have been here all along, but I've been too afraid to come out." Bianca looked over at him with her aloof fashion as if to say, "I knew you were there all along." I was so happy to see him! I hugged him and kissed him and we've taken care of him from that day forward. When I ran out and left the front door open, he ran into my apartment. Somehow Cosho knew that this was where Bianca lived and felt safe going there.

Well, two months later Bianca and Cosho moved with me to a big fancy home that I was having built on the lake in a very nice neighborhood. Cosho had gotten more than he was looking for. He lived like a king in a big home and had all the toys, love, and affection he could hope for. There were a couple of Busters in the neighborhood, but then again, there was his best friend Bianca. Bianca acted aloof towards

Cosho, which was her demeanor, but when it came time to defend him she was always there, looking out for him. As I said, Cosho was a lover and a talker, not a fighter.

Seven years after our introduction that day on the sidewalk, and after his rescue from the elements and the Busters of this world, Cosho died of leukemia. He had the heart of a kind and gentle angel from heaven. A great creature made by God with a sweet heart and the friendliest disposition. He had two friends who loved him and protected him all his life. When Cosho died I could see that Bianca missed her best friend as much as I do.

Cosho: Male Cat (American Indian Language)

Cosho

Bianca

Taylor & Klassen

Blind Baby Magoo

Logan Grey
Savannah, GA

For a little over a year now my heart and attention have been stolen by the most precious kitty alive. His name is Magoo and he very nearly died in my backyard. This time last year he was living under my boyfriend's house with his two siblings and mother. They came out at night to eat from the food dish we put out for strays. At one time we had seven cats eating outside, not counting the two cats that we already owned. Most of the outside cats were too shy to come close enough for us to pet them, but too hungry to stay away for long.

Every time the young mother saw me coming, she and three striped kittens would bolt in the other direction. The little gray kitten with white sock feet was slower than the others and often ran along the fence before disappearing underneath it. I didn't realize it at the time, but the fence was how he marked his surroundings. One night my boyfriend Tadd was walking around the pool and came up behind the gray kitten before it realized he was there. As soon as "Gray Baby," which is what he'd begun calling it, became aware of Tadd's presence he shot forward launching himself straight into the pool. Tadd immediately fished him out and as soon as he was on dry land again, he ran away spitting and hissing.

Gray Baby fell in the pool again three days later, but no one was outside to see him fall in this time. It was July 4th and Tadd and I were inside watching television. We'd already eaten our burgers and launched our fireworks. He turned to me, "Do you hear something?"

I listened for a second. "No, I don't think so," I said.

"There's a strange noise coming from outside," he persisted and then went to check it out.

I didn't think much of it as he's always hearing imaginary noises outside. This time, when he went to investigate the noise he came back with a terrified and soaking wet Gray Baby. His eyes were wide with fear and he was still trying to swim even as Tadd held him. The kitten was so shocked he forgot to be afraid of us. I wrapped him in a towel and held him on the couch trying to calm him. There was no telling how long he'd been treading water in the pool.

I spoke to him softly trying to earn his trust and ruffled his downy gray fur in an attempt to dry him. His tiny heart beat frantically in that perfect white furred chest. Once he was sufficiently dry I placed him back outside and let him go with his family. His mother was outside anxiously waiting for him.

A few days later I thought better of the decision to put him back outside. I was able to sneak up behind Gray Baby and capture him with little resistance. Once inside he seemed perfectly okay with just sitting on my lap. When I sat him down on the floor he immediately went to a corner and stared at the wall. He paced in a small area and cried. After he bumped headfirst into the doorframe, we realized the problem. He was totally blind.

It was soon decided. Neither of us could bear the thought of another pool accident or worse. How could he escape if a bigger unfriendly animal chased him? We purchased kitten food and litter for the weekend. Tadd decided we would call him "Magoo" after the blind cartoon character.

The first few days Magoo didn't try to explore the house and barely ate anything. I offered him dry food, wet food and even "cat milk." He curled into a ball in the corner of my bedroom and slept on a little blue baby blanket. While awake, he walked around the perimeter of my room and cried non-stop no matter what I did. I tried to get him to sleep in my bed. I even let him lay on my chest, but there was no comfort for him. I began to worry that my decision to take him away from his mother hadn't been the right one. It was three full nights before he managed to sleep without crying.

It was nearly a week into his adoption before Magoo became comfortable with his new surroundings. He had previously disregarded all the toys we'd given him and displayed none of the typical wild kitten energy I was expecting to see. I was at a loss for what to do to make him happy. He didn't seem interested in anything until the day he walked up to my bedroom door and tried to climb it. He furiously attacked the door and swatted at the open air. I was overjoyed at this positive sign and promptly gave him a pair of my panty hose to play with. That day I realized I would have sacrificed a dozen pairs of hose to see Magoo happy.

His adoption date is fast approaching and I'm reminded of how much progress he's made. His vet told us that he had congenital blindness in one eye and the other was likely damaged due to head trauma. His eyes are still perfect looking and when he turns his head to hear you better it looks as if he can see you.

"He'll never be able to see his mommy," Tadd said one day.

I was undaunted by this statement. "He sees me with his heart," I replied.

In my eyes Magoo couldn't be any more perfect. He still bonks his little nose on furniture sometimes but he shakes it off and keeps going. He has grown taller than the scratching post I bought him as a kitten but still loves to attack it. He's happy playing with a paper grocery bag or his cat toys. My older male cat, Ghetto, enjoys having a playmate and wrestles Magoo around the living room.

I'm always excited when he discovers something new, whether it is that tree in the front yard, or the fact that he likes cheese popcorn. When we first got Magoo he couldn't even get on the couch without help, and now he can scale the side of his 6ft cat tower with ease. He doesn't go through the middle but climbs the side of the tower and then scoots back down tail first.

He sleeps at my feet every night and his beautiful gray face is the first thing I see every morning. His presence gives me comfort and encouragement. When he's sitting in the window watching for me to come home in the afternoon, my heart melts. I have a necklace with his baby picture inside, and since I can't take him with me always, I wear the necklace to cheer myself. Magoo has brought a lot of joy and love into our home. I'm so thankful to have him.

Magoo

Taylor & Klassen

Ugly the Cat

A Well-Known Story by an
Unknown Author

WARNING:

THIS STORY CONTAINS EMOTIONALLY DISTURBING CONTENT!

Everyone in the housing complex I lived in knew who Ugly was. Ugly was the resident stray cat. Ugly loved three things in this world: fighting, eating garbage, and... Love. The combination of these things, combined with a life spent outside, had their effect on Ugly.

To start with, he had only one eye, and where the other should have been was a gaping hole. He was also missing his ear on the same side, his left foot has appeared to have been badly broken at one time, and had healed at an unnatural angle, making him look like he was always turning the corner. His tail had long been lost, leaving only the smallest stub, which he would constantly jerk and twitch. Ugly would have been a dark gray tabby, except for the sores covering his head, neck, even his shoulders with thick, yellowing scabs. Every time someone saw Ugly there was the same reaction. "That's one UGLY cat!!"

All the children were warned not to touch him. The adults threw rocks at him, hosed him down, and squirted him when he tried to come in their homes, or shut his paws in the door when he would not leave. Ugly always had the same reaction. If you turned the hose on him, he would stand there, getting soaked until you gave up and quit. If you threw things at him, he would curl his lanky body around his feet in forgiveness.

Whenever he spied children, he would come running meowing frantically and bump his head against their hands, begging for their love. If you ever picked him up he would immediately begin licking on your shirt, earrings, whatever he could find.

One day Ugly shared his love with the neighbor's huskies. They did not respond kindly, and Ugly was badly mauled. From my house I could hear his screams, and I tried to rush to his aid. By the time I got to where he was laying, it was apparent Ugly's sad life was almost at an end. Ugly lay in a wet circle, his back legs and lower back twisted grossly out of shape, a gaping tear in the white strip of fur that ran down his front.

As I picked him up and tried to carry him home I could hear him wheezing and gasping, and could feel him struggling. It must be hurting him terribly, I thought. Then I felt a familiar tugging, sucking sensation on my ear. Ugly, in so much pain, suffering, and obviously dying was trying to lick my ear. I pulled him closer to me, and he bumped the palm of my hand with his head, then he turned his one golden eye towards me, and I could hear the distinct sound of purring. Even in the greatest pain, that ugly battled-scarred cat was asking only for a little affection, and perhaps some compassion.

At that moment I thought Ugly was the most beautiful, loving creature I had ever seen. Never once did he try to bite or scratch me, or even try to get away from me, or struggle in any way. Ugly just looked up at me completely trusting in me to relieve his pain. Ugly died in my arms before I could get inside, but I sat and held him for a long time afterwards, thinking about how one scared, deformed little stray could so alter my opinion about what it means to have true pureness of spirit, to love so totally and truly.

Ugly was buried under an old oak tree, in a small plot bordered by daisies. His small plaque reads: *Love is Eternal.* Every day when I walked past it, I would tell him I loved him.

Ugly taught me more about giving and compassion than a thousand books, lectures, or talk show specials ever could, and for that I will always be thankful. He had been scarred on the outside, but I was scarred on the inside, and it was time for me to learn to love truly and deeply, to give my total to those I cared for.

Many people want to be richer, more successful, well liked or beautiful.......but for me, I will always try to be Ugly.

Taylor & Klassen

MOO

Aaron Horwath
Portland, OR

I had been sent out into the field on a mission; a game of whiffle-ball had landed the ball somewhere amongst the high grass, and as the oldest in the group playing, I was designated as the most-fit individual for the reconnaissance mission. I had made my way in a quick climb up and over our backyard fence, and moments after landing, found myself in the empty field. Finding a white ball amongst high yellow grass is a difficult task, and one that I knew would take time, but I willingly began my search.

I searched for a while, how long I did not know. The only sound to accompany me was the light electrical whisper of a power line that ran above me. The grass below my feet was crisp in the summer sun, and crunched, ironically, much like a light snow-pack, a sound reminiscent of the previous December. I knew the general vicinity in which the ball had landed, and had been, as best I could, systematically searching for the ball, walking back and forth, head down, being careful to keep my focus on the task at hand.

As I began to acknowledge that I may return to my backyard empty-handed, I heard a rustling a few feet from where I stood. I stopped and listened. The grass rustled again. My first thought was that it might be a snake. I knew if it were a snake it would only be a harmless garter, but my body responded as though I might be in for a fight for my life. Sweat began to gather around my brow, my breathing grew short, my limbs immovable.

But I would not worry long. As I stood, the grass rustled once again, but this time it was accompanied by the most comforting sound I could have imagined: a tiny *meow.*

It was a kitten!

The tension in my body relaxed, I wiped the sweat from my brow, and released a long and necessary sigh. I walked carefully towards the rustling grass, not sure exactly where the kitten was and not wanting to accidentally crush it underfoot. After a few feet, the grass parted slightly, and at the center of the small clearing was the smallest kitten I had ever seen. It looked up at me and released as emphatic a *meow* as it could muster, clearly distressed at its situation. I quickly scanned its body for injuries, and when I determined there were none, I devised a plan. I found a large stick a few feet from the kitten and stuck it in the ground near its place to mark its spot. I then quickly returned to my home, grabbed a shoebox and the members of my family, and we made our way out to make a rescue.

Our family had fostered kittens before for animal shelters in our area, so we were relatively familiar with the necessary steps that needed to be taken if we wanted to make our rescued kitten the newest member of our family. After a trip to a veterinarian and a chat with the head of a local animal shelter, as well as a short family conference to do a little parental convincing, we excitedly welcomed the kitten into our family as a permanent member.

Flash-forward a few years. The kitten which I had found in the grass has grown up to be a 22 pound Maine Coon that now goes by the name Moo. Abandoned early on by her mother for reasons unknown, Moo was raised by my significantly smaller dog, Makai, a 5 pound Maltese-Poodle. For Moo's first few years of life, she learned all the necessary skills for being a successful pet living in suburbia from Makai, and their friendship lasted until Makai's death in 2012.

Though Makai has passed away, Moo continues life as a healthy cat, and carries on many dog-like characteristics learned from her days growing up with Makai. From her love of belly rubs, to ringing a bell when she needs to use the bathroom, to her warm welcomes as she bounds towards me upon my arrival home, Moo has grown up to be a cat with a strong persona. She will always carry with her the memories of Makai, and is 22 pounds of fur, fun, and love.

Moo

Maggie & Maya

Lisa Gallarini
Charlotte, NC

In January of 2013 I went to color a friend's hair, and when I went to the bathroom there was a small kitten curled up in the bathtub. I tried to pet her but she hissed at me. I looked over and noticed she did not have any water or food. I got some fresh water and put it in the bowl, then gently reached over to get her and place her in front of the water bowl. She drank that water like she had not had any in days. I was puzzled that my friend had a kitten in this condition in her bathroom so I asked her what was going on with the tiny kitten. She looked to be about 5-6 weeks old. My friend told me that sometimes her husband lets the dog in the house and it seems the dog was not so nice to the kitten. Also, they had a 1 year old that did not know how to handle the kitten, and I imagine the kitten had scratched her. The poor kitten had gotten a prison sentence in the bathroom. This person was known for getting animals and then no longer wanting them when she realized that animals can be a lot of work.

I got home that January night and all I could think about was this little white kitten with grey eyes. I asked my husband what he thought, and he told me to do whatever I felt was right. I called my friend and asked her if she really wanted the kitten. She quickly replied. "No." I asked if I could come get her and she said, "YES!" We actually met in the Target parking lot and I came home with my little rescue bundle. I honestly had no plans of keeping her because I already had two 13 year old calico cats. I also have a Quaker parrot, and a lion head rabbit. The last thing I wanted was another cat. My plan was to get her healthy with all of her shots so that I could find her a home. I called rescue shelters and everyone was full. The longer I had the kitten, the more I realized she would not make a great pet to anyone with kids or other animals. She hid under anything she could and was scared to death of people. She almost seemed like a feral cat. Then I noticed on her belly she was covered with fleas. I ran out and got her some meds and quarantined her to my bathroom until the fleas were gone. I made her a bed and got her some good food for kittens. She ate well and the fleas were gone, but still no sign of affection towards another living creature. Her eyes seemed dilated most of the time as if she were spooked. I started to wonder if there was anything else wrong with her. I figured the best I could do was love her unconditionally. I had hoped if I could get her better I would one day find her a home.

Then May 2013 came, and I still had the little white kitten I had named "Maggie". I often sing the Rod Stewart song to her. "Wake up Maggie I think I got something to say to you." She looks at me as if I am the one with the problem. Funny girl. Anyway, here comes May, and my friend called me to tell me she found a little black kitten in the road. I knew the issues Maggie had and I honestly did not want the same thing to happen to this little black kitty. I quickly went over and picked up the box with the little black puff ball inside. She was so tiny and so sweet. I thought for sure I could find this one a good home. As soon as I got her home I took pictures, even ones with a little yellow flower over her ear. My calicos were hissing at her as though to say, "Oh heck no, this is not happening again." I had to tell them to be nice and share the love, that this little one would not be here long. I told the calico girls, Bella and Zoe that the only reason Maggie was still here was until we worked on her trust issues. So, here I am with three small children, two 13 year old calico cats, a parrot, a rabbit, and two small rescue kittens that needed good homes. So what do I do? I name the little black kitten! May is my anniversary month and my favorite spiritual teacher is Maya Angelou. Maya it shall be. So here I sit with Maggie and Maya, two totally different personalities. My children could pick Maya up like a rag doll and put her in any position they pleased, but they could not go near Maggie. You could burp and Maggie would dart as if a torpedo was about to hit. Any sound freaks her out, and in this house, all you get is sound. Someone is laughing, crying, running, jumping, singing, or dancing in this house at all times. Seeing this little kitten so traumatized and untrusting just broke my heart.

I had already listed Maya to find a good home for her, and had gotten some replies. Funny things happen when you start to get attached. It seems no one was good enough for my little Maya. I was making excuses to keep her here. My kids seemed to adore her and she seemed to feel mutually about them. So, I did what any smart person would do, and took the listing down. Welcome home Maya.

Maggie was a different story. She was always hiding and afraid. No matter how hard I tried, it seemed I could not get through to her. I posted a listing to see if I could find someone for my special needs kitty. I wanted someone who did not have children or maybe someone who was alone and quiet. I got one reply and that was it. No one wanted my special needs kitty, and I was honest about how she was. The last thing I needed was her to go to a home and be traumatized all over again. The lady asked about shots and disease and I told her I could not get her into a carrier to take her to the vet. I told her if she wanted her I would pay to have her spayed and get her shots and a good checkup. She never replied back. Then it hit me, if I cannot even get her into a carrier, how will I introduce her to a new owner. How would they get her home?

Then, guess what my husband and I did? We got a German shepherd puppy in October 2013. I know what you're thinking. A zoo, right. Crazy? Yes and yes. We were totally asking for punishment. We did not have a crate the first week for the puppy, so she slept on the couch. One night she managed to come into my room and jump on the bed. I woke up to the most awful hiss and my hand was slit wide open. It was Maggie, she had been sleeping with us and I had no idea. This little kitten that had not wanted anything to do with anyone had been sleeping with us. That was the first sign I saw of her making a connection. I did not know whether to scream in pain from my wounded hand, or scream for joy. I did both. I still have a scar on my hand.

We got the puppy her crate, but as much as I thought it was so great that Maggie had been sleeping with us, it seems the puppy encounter threw her right back to totally freaked out. I felt like the biggest idiot. How could I have a kitten who was wounded by a dog in her first few weeks of life and now I bring a puppy into my home? What was I thinking? Then one day an amazing thing happened. Maggie let me pick her up and kiss her cheek! I told her she was safe with me and she'd never have to worry. Before I knew it, if I would lie still enough in my bed she would come lay beside me and let me gently pet her. I could not be happier. This little diluted calico girl was learning to trust.

Going back, I had originally scheduled Maggie and Maya to be spayed on the same day. It did not go as planned. I could shove Maya in a mason jar if I wanted, but Maggie was not going anywhere. My husband exhausted himself and no matter how hard we tried, we could not get her into a carrier. He used welders' gloves so he was not shredded like cheese. She popped out of that carrier like lightning. He was out of time and had to get Maya to her appointment.

Maya did just fine and has now doubled her size. She is beautiful and just a joy. I finally called the clinic to get some tips. We scheduled Maggie for the next day, and I knew this was my last chance to get her fixed so that she could stay with us. The first box I got her in was a rescue box we use to transport injured raptors. Maggie busted out of the bottom and disappeared. I felt defeated and was covered in sweat. But, I was determined to get this little girl fixed. I finally got her and put her in a carrier that she could not bust out of and got her to the clinic. I picked her up later that day and she was drunk as a cooter. I got a small office ready so she could recover. She once again hid for several days and wanted nothing to do with anyone. I figured she was mad at me. I told her I was sorry and that I had to do it so I could keep her forever. After a few days, she walked up to my 7 year old and let her pet her. This was the best ever. She loves my kids!! This is huge! After another few days she was back out and lounging on the bed and chair in my room. I can lay with her and love her. The whole family, except poor Rozie, the shepherd, can love her. She is home now and she is loved.

A rough start and a relationship I never knew would exist. It took work on both of our parts, but now she is with me, and I am with her. Recently, Maya Angelou passed and I am happy to have my little Maya to remind me of how great the world can still be. And that is how Maggie and Maya came home to us.

Maggie

Maya

Giter

Rowie Martinez
Toronto, Ontario

None of us kids really knew where the thing came from. The tiny, black kitten was just suddenly there in the middle of the living room, mewling and leaving muddy paw prints on the pristine waxed floor. Its eyes were almost shut, oozing with yellowish sickness. My aunt said it swam through the ghastly floodwaters caused by Super Typhoon Rita and into their house; it was raining cats and dogs that entire week after all. As if to prove her point, the kitten smelled of sewage. So naturally, none of us wanted anything to do with it. It was not cute and would probably die soon.

My aunt tried to sweep it out of the house with her straw broom. With reflexes it looked like it didn't have, the kitten darted under the heavy couch and hissed at her attempts to get it out. Her two children tried to help her by making faces and screaming at it. My younger brother and I watched them, laughing loudly, cheering for the ball of wet dirt that was their opponent.

"Go! Go, muck-ball! Wooo! Kill that broom!"

"Enough of that, all of you!" commanded my grandmother as she made her way down the curved staircase. Stern family matriarch, the queen of clean and the sewing machine, she was the one we least expected to be on the animal's side.

"We have to get it out. It's filthy and probably rabid! It might die in here." cried my aunt as she continued to poke the kitten with her broom.

"Better in here than out there." replied grandmother, gesturing at the violent rain and winds outside wreaking havoc on Manila. To us kids, she said "You can have it for a pet."

We glanced at each other in silence. My aunt audibly sighed. Not one of us liked the idea of having it as a pet.

"Psss...psss...psss...ming...ming...ming..." Grandma imitated the sounds of the kitten, but with a gentle tone that calmed even us. She got down on her knees to look under the couch, but the kitten was no longer there.

They said Grandma found the kitten a few days later in the small closet on the stairs' landing, where my father's childhood comic book collection was stored. It had wedged itself in the farthest, darkest corner, safe from us children. I was not happy about this. That closet was my favorite spot in their house. Reading the comic books would take me to places like London and Paris where two guys looked alike, or to Russia where brothers with unpronounceable names lived and did things I did not understand, or in some strange place in the future where firemen burned books. It was MY place. Now the demon-kitten had claimed it.

"Grandma, I want the kitten out of my closet." I openly declared my disdain for it.

"Don't mind him, he only sleeps there." she said. "Leave him alone. Do not try to touch him."

She led me back to the stairs' landing, a saucer of milk in her dainty hand. She opened the closet door and carefully reached in to place down the saucer where the kitten was already hissing. As soon as she set it down, the kitten swiped a paw at her. Grandma yelped and quickly withdrew her hand. I saw deep scratches on her thumb and they were bleeding.

I watched as Grandma patched up her hand, feeling even more loathing for the creature in the closet.

"Ah, he's getting stronger! Good. Next time, I'll bring him some steamed fish as a treat. I'm going to try to clean him up a bit soon. He's not going to like that!" It surprised me that she sounded pleased that the kitten got her good. I noticed that her other hand had bandages on them and a few spots dabbed with Mercurochrome. So, it had been a while she had been doing this, feeding the kitten and getting clawed for her effort.

It was several weeks later when I visited their house. To my delight, the kitten had vacated the closet and I was free to again travel to those exotic comic book places I so loved.

"Grandma, it's gone! The kitten is gone!" I cheerfully informed her as I burst into her bedroom.

She greeted me with a smile and waved me in. She was reclining on her favorite chair, reading a large book with picture of a cat on the cover. There were several other cat books on top of her side table. On her lap was a skinny tabby kitten, its clean, grey fur lined with vivid stripes. Its tail though, looked like it was dipped in tar. It still had a funny smell.

"Is that it? Is that the muck-ball that came in from the storm?" I wondered aloud.

"Yes, it is. Isn't he cute?"

I had to admit, it was now looking kind of cute. I reached out to pet it but the kitten was having none of that. It hissed and swiped its paws at me. If I wasn't fast enough, I would have received a bloody souvenir.

"He is getting stronger every day with some milk, fish and lots of love. I think he's ready for some meat, too. I wish I could afford a vet to look at him, though. His eyes still look a little cloudy. I named him Giter." She tickled the kitten's chin as she said this, as if talking to it instead of me. "And later this week, Giter will have his first bath and we'll see what to do about his tail! Isn't that right, Giter?"

"Giter, gutter, goiter – call him whatever. I'll ask dad if I can bring home his comics so I don't have to..."

"It's Giter, because he looks like a tiny tiger, but not really." Grandma cut me off, giggling at her own joke.

The rainy season continued on and that year rolled over to the next. We kids did things that kids do. I paid no more mind to my Grandmother's nursing of that kitten. I had more important things to do, trees to climb, anime to watch, boys to beat up and of course, classes to attend. It was a good ten months later, at least, when I visited Grandma's house again.

Running up the stairs to get to Grandma's room, I was surprised to see a regal-looking grey tabby, pawing the closet door open. My grandma descended the stairs behind the cat, a big smile on her face.

"Giter has a present for us." She peered inside the closet, not opening it all the way.

With all the bravado of a 9-year-old, I flung the doors open and beheld the cutest sight of life. In place of my comics was a cardboard box, lined with flannel and full of squirming kittens. Four of them, all healthy and cute!

"Giter is female; I didn't realize that until her first vet visit." said Grandma.

"Wow..." was all I could say. My heart melted.

It was apparent by the way she looked at me that Giter did not approve of my gawking at her babies. However, she purred when Grandma reached over and touched the curious M pattern on her forehead.

"M for muck-ball, then miracle and now, mother, too." and she giggled again.

Taylor & Klassen

Who Saved Who?

Joel Mozgiel
Vancouver, B.C.

If you would have asked me two years ago if I would like to own a cat, I would have looked at you like you had two heads and one of them was painted orange. But, life is a funny thing and the world is a funny place where funny things happen to funny people. Now when I say funny, I mean strange.

I had closed the restaurant that night. It was mid-October and I was surprised that it wasn't raining from every direction. It had been another long day of many long days which were slowly piling up to become a very long year. I was exhausted, miserable, bored, dejected, antisocial, ill tempered, over-worked, underpaid, shut in, burnt out, fed up and low down. Slowly walking home, I was alone under a moody canopy of low hanging clouds, kicking a soggy old stick along the cold damp sidewalk.

I recognized my troubles. I took a big draw of the stale night air and uttered "I just need something new in my life!" under a foggy breath. I put my head down and began cycling through thoughts on how I was going to dig my way out of this hollow pit I was in.

I was about three blocks from my place. All I wanted was a hot shower and a cold beer. Anything to distract me from the perpetual ugly thoughts boiling away in my head. There I was, storming along, oblivious to everything around me, completely lost in my own relentless funk. Then as if from straight out of thin air, a black cat rushed across the sidewalk in front of me. I froze where I stood. "I must be damned!" gasped the beastly voice in my head. "That's all I need!" My head fell back, and I faced the sinister skies developing above me. I honestly thought that some unholy lightning bolt was going to reap me right out of my shoes.

I slowly exhaled and opened one eye after the other. I peeked around and saw that everything was calm. My vivid imagination seemed to have created a blanket of paranoia that granted me a moment of clarity from my restless mind. At my feet was a cat on its back staring up at me, squeaking in its own language. Its fur was so black it looked blue, its huge green eyes stood out like a neon light. I acknowledged the cat, but I was dubious to touch it. I did not want it to follow me. It was superstition coupled with my own mix of make-believe and rage that were preventing me from seeing what was actually happening here.

I politely stepped over the cat and continued making quick steps back to my place. It was right on my heels. I picked up the pace. It weaved between my steps with the agility and grace of a ninja that practiced ballet on the weekends. At the end of the block, I stopped. The cat swooped its tail and tried to sidle into my legs. I took a step back and said, "You must live around here. Now, you can't follow me any longer 'cause

I don't know if you'll find your way back. So go on!" I clapped my hands loudly and it darted off into a hedge. I turned around and didn't look back. I didn't have to. It was already waiting for me by the time I got to the other side of the street. "Okay, suit yourself. I tried to warn you and I can't take care of you, so once I get to the door you're on your own." I couldn't believe I was trying to reason with a cat. We walked another two blocks. She was nipping at my shoelaces as they swung in between steps and rolling onto her back and chirping sweet little sounds. She knew what she was doing. I was having trouble coming to terms with it, but that little black kitty was melting the ice cave that I had become lost in.

I finally found the first bit of light that cracked through and admitted to myself that I liked her. But I had to be fair and reasonable. You can't just take a cat. What if she belonged to someone who loved her? She's not feral, she's sweet and friendly like no other cat I've ever seen before and there was no denying it, she was a beauty. Besides, I've never had a cat before. I don't know how to care for a cat. The only pet I ever had was a hamster when I was a young boy, and I took its cage outside in the summertime and the poor thing fried in the sun. I'm not good with pets. I have enough problems already. She has to belong to someone. I came to the tough conclusion that I could not keep her.

I headed towards the basement door, she went to explore the patio upstairs. Okay, here's my chance to make a break for it. Quick and painless. "Good night kitty cat! Thanks for walking me home." I rushed in the door just as fresh rain began to freckle the damp concrete. I took off my jacket, snapped open a beer and drained half of it. I headed for the shower, but before I could run the water; I felt hollow. My mind raced back through the tense network of emotions that I'd recently been feeding off and neglecting. Back to a half an ago and the cold breath I took when I said, "Something new".

I threw on my robe and sneakers, pulled open the door and looked out at the rainy street. I scanned the dark small spots in the lane way for something small and dark. I had that desperate feeling, like a brick is lodged in your chest and your heart beats heavily trying to loosen it. Until I spotted her. The rain had painted the small guiltless cat into a dry corner under the steps. It was so dark that I could only see two big round eyes that flickered odd looks of both sorrow and joy. She walked over to me twisting her tail into the shape of a question mark and offered a pleading sound. I put my hand out and she ran her face along it, I scratched behind her ear which made her wink. She was cool and soft with tiny drops of rain sparkling in her flossy coat. I ran my hand from her neck through her tail, smudging them into her dark silky coat. I picked her up and held her to my shoulder, swaddling her tiny cold paws in my robe. She was purring so I could hear it and her big "Granny Smith" eyes blinked into slits. We faced each other closely and seemed to make some kind of unspoken vow. It was one of those many, special moments when yesterday and tomorrow seem a million miles away.

She entered the apartment easily and began to explore the many corners. I got down on my knees to connect with her. I gently grabbed the scruff of her neck and massaged her into what seemed like a paralyzed state. I was sure that she was a female but I checked to be sure. I checked her over for fleas, mange, matted hair, any kind of wounds. She seemed a bit thin, but she was clean and healthy as far as I could tell. I tore a sheet of paper from my notebook and rolled it into a ball which seized all of her attention. I tossed it up in the air and spiked it into the corner of the room. She shot after it like it was tethered to her. She swatted and chased after it from one end of the room to the other and back again. That would keep her busy. I took the opportunity to counsel with the great minds of the internet for any advice or information to help us out.

It was too late to go to the store, so I fed her a bit of canned tuna and set out a cup of water. I made her a bed in the laundry room out of spare towels. I had all the bases covered except for kitty litter. I was just going to have to take that chance until the morning came. We smiled and purred and played with the paper ball until we were both yawning. I lead her into the laundry room and closed the door behind us. I let her patrol the room until she found the pile of towels. I took a knee as she began to work them to her satisfaction, warming them up to take her rest. She nestled in and curled up. I scratched her softly behind her ears and along the edges of her face until she melted off. I took a moment to adore her. I thought about my walk home and how I felt so far away from that now. I would never have thought that this was what I needed. I would have never allowed myself to make the conscious decision to keep a cat. It was only because of the circumstance, because she chose me. It was the spooky kind of miracle that allows you believe in fairy tales.

For the next 2 weeks I was apprehensive to read any poster I saw on a lamp post or telephone pole. I was reluctant, but I did report her "found" to the SPCA. They were glad when I did and they hadn't had any calls from anybody looking for her, so I was glad too. After a few weeks passed. I took her to the vet and had her checked out properly. They assessed her to be close to a year old, she had not been spayed, and she was confirmed to be one of the softest cats around. It had started to feel like the two of us were going to be alright together. It was time to give her a name. I'd been so worried that I wouldn't be able to keep her that I refused to name her. I had one in my mind though. Based on the eerie serendipity of how that little black cat found me when I was so troubled and lonely, and that it was about a week or so before Halloween. I thought that "Spooky" would suit her well.

There is a very noticeable difference now that I have her around. She's pretty independent and doesn't require a lot of attention. She greets me when I arrive and sees me off when I leave. We have this little plush ducky on a string. I get a kick out of dragging it across the carpet and watching her go after it. Whether she's silently stalking it or wildly attacking it like it disgraced her family, it's fun for both of us. We call that one "Spooky the Terror Cat vs. The Dead Duck". Sometimes she's very curious and has to get her little nose right into whatever I'm doing. Other times she just perches on top of the fridge and watches me fix supper. A lot of the time she likes to make me jealous and just sit in the window watching the world go by. She doesn't always come to bed with me, but typically I will find her gratefully sleeping at my feet when I wake. Having a cat around the place adds some character, some warmth, some richness to my life. It keeps me from living inside of my head. It makes being alone not feel lonely. When I think about it, some of the most amazing lessons in life come from the most unexpected teachers.

Spooky

A SPECIAL STORY FOR CHILDREN

The Amazing Ralphie

Written & Illustrated
By

Katrina Duesterhaus
El Segundo, CA

It was a warm spring day when we first met. On a trip to the grocery store, I noticed a lady and her daughter trying to feed a kitten in the parking lot.

"Where did that kitty come from?" I asked.

"I don't know, it was just here," they told me.

They put the food out for the kitten before leaving. I did my shopping and left too, but I couldn't help thinking about that kitty in the parking lot.

It looked so tiny, where was its mother? And summer was approaching. Soon the asphalt would become hot and burn the soft skin on the kitten's paws.

I was worried and I wanted to do something but I knew I needed help.

Luckily I knew an organization that specialized in kitty rescue. I had worked with Purrfect Partners about 6 months earlier to rescue a litter of feral kittens living near a plant nursery.

Around sunrise the next day I went back with a special box called a trap. Traps are used to rescue wild animals without hurting them. I put some food inside the trap, and when the kitten went inside to eat, the door shut behind it.

Now in the trap, I had a chance to see the kitten up close and I could tell it was a boy. I decided to call him Ralphie, since I found him at Ralph's grocery store.

That's when I saw something else. There was a little problem. He had a bubble on his belly that wasn't supposed to be there.

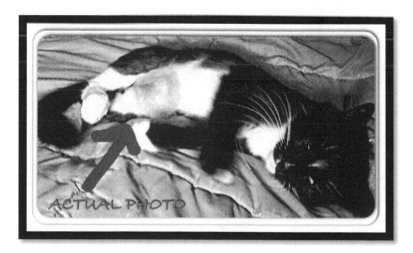

Normally rescue kittens are immediately taken to a Spay and Neuter clinic. At the clinic, the veterinarian makes a tiny change on the animal's body so they don't have babies. This change is called spaying for girls, and neutering for boys.

Because of the bubble on Ralphie's belly I wanted to take him to see a special veterinarian doctor. So Ralphie came home with me that day while I worked with Purrfect Partners to get him an appointment with the specialist. That night I cleaned him up, filled his belly, and gave him lots of love.

Boy was he happy!

The next day Ralphie and I went to see Dr. Liebl in Hermosa Beach, California. He took a picture of the insides of Ralphie's body.

The X-Ray showed that the bubble was something called an umbilical hernia. Dr. Liebl knew he had to remove the hernia with surgery so Ralphie could get better.

The surgery only took a couple of hours, and after that I was able to bring Ralphie back home. When Ralphie came home, he was really tired from his surgery and pretty much slept all the rest of that day and night.

Ralphie had to wear a bandage on his belly and a cone on his head. Animals in the wild use licking as a way to clean their wounds. Over thousands of years animals have learned that if it hurts, lick it, and it will usually get better.

Dr. Liebl knew Ralphie would want to lick it, so Ralphie wore a cone that went all around his face to block his tongue from licking his healing belly.

The next day he met the other kittens, who were very curious about him. They thought he looked strange with his bandage shirt and cone head.

At dinner time Ralphie's cone actually became an advantage as he pushed the other kittens away from their plates and ate their food.

In a couple days the bandage came off and the other kittens finally started to see Ralphie as a cat too. A couple weeks later his belly was all better and the cone came off!

He really was just like the other kitties! They all became friends and now will live happy ever after together.

Ralphie and White Sox are best friends and they love to cuddle!

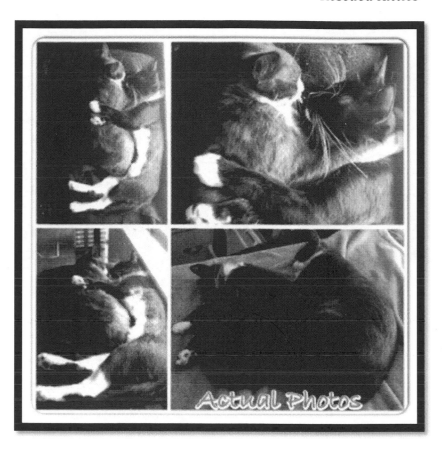

36306781R00060

Made in the USA
San Bernardino, CA
19 July 2016